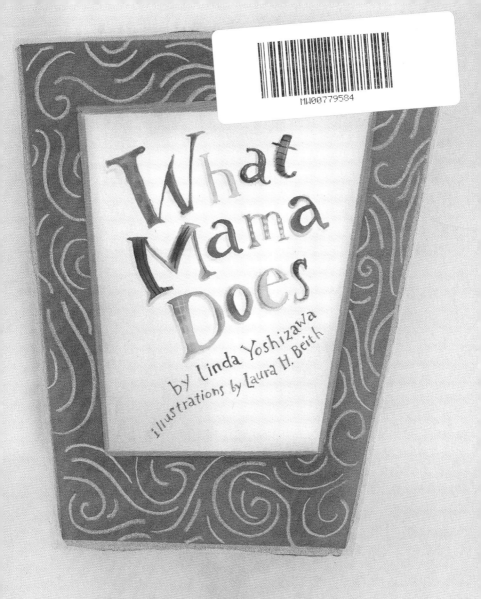

What Mama Does

by Linda Yoshizawa

illustrations by Laura H. Beith

MODERN CURRICULUM PRESS
Pearson Learning Group

Friday started out like any other school day. Right after lunch, Mrs. Novak reminded the class about Career Week.

"Don't forget that you won't have to come to school on Monday," Mrs. Novak began.

The class cheered, and Mia winked at her best friend Beth.

"Monday is the first day of Career Week," Mrs. Novak went on. "As you know, we've been planning a long time for this. Instead of coming to school, you'll be going to work with an adult family member or friend. Then you'll write a report about what you learned. We'll spend the rest of the week sharing your reports."

This time Mia didn't look at Beth. She looked across the room at her twin brother, Ricky. Ricky looked the way she felt—glum.

Everyone else in the class seemed to be buzzing with excitement.

"My mom is the mayor, so maybe I'll get to run the city."

"I can't wait to spend a whole day at the fire station."

"I'll bet you wish you could work in the emergency clinic with my dad and me."

On the way home, Mia and Ricky talked about Monday.

"Career Week is no big deal!" Ricky muttered. "You and I will go to the store. As if that will be big news! Everybody goes to the store all the time. At least our report will be easy to write. I've got mine written already: Our mom's a good mom, and a really nice person. But she doesn't do much. She just works in a store. The end."

Mama's attitude was just the opposite of Mia and Ricky's. She was as excited as the class had been.

"It's been a long time since you accompanied me to the store," Mama said, "and this time you'll be starting in the morning and staying the whole day! There's so much for you to see and do. I can't wait!

"You know," Mama went on, "I wasn't much older than you two when I first started working at the store. I remember the day I filled out my application. I was so afraid of rejection that I paced back and forth in front of the store for a whole hour. But they felt I was qualified, and they hired me right away. I was so proud when I took my first paycheck home to your grandmother. Even though I was still in high school, I felt so independent."

Mama sighed. "Back then, I had other plans. I didn't expect to work in the store my whole life. But I liked working there, and I kept getting promotions." Mama brightened. "Anyway, I really love my career, and I can't wait to share it with you two!"

Mia and Ricky knew they just couldn't hurt Mama's feelings. They couldn't let her know they wished she had a more exciting job.

Over the weekend both Mia and Ricky dreamed about Career Day. Mia dreamed Mama was a surgeon. Mia was handing Mama tools as she performed a life-saving operation. Then Mia dreamed that Mama was a circus performer. She was flying through the air on a high trapeze. Mia jumped from another trapeze. Mama caught her with a big smile. The audience cheered.

Ricky dreamed that Mama was the only woman laborer on a big construction project. Proudly wearing his hard hat, he followed Mama up tall ladders. They walked across beams that were high in the air. By the end of the dream, they were both covered with grime. But they smiled as they looked at the huge building they had built together in a single day. Then he dreamed that she was a race car driver. He rode beside her as she careened around steeply banked turns. He stood by as she modestly accepted her trophy.

Their dreams ended when Mama woke them Monday morning at six o'clock.

"The store doesn't open until ten," Ricky grumbled, as he blinked in the strong light. "Why do we have to leave so early?"

"The customers don't come until ten," Mama replied. "But a lot happens before the store opens."

A security guard met them in the parking lot at a quarter to seven. Mama unlocked the door and locked it again behind them. As the guard walked them upstairs to the offices, Mia and Ricky looked around. Even though they'd shopped in the store all their lives, they wouldn't have known it now. Only a few night lights were on.

The store was full of spooky shadows, and mannequins seemed to jump out as Ricky and Mia walked by.

Just inside the office door Mama stopped in front of a panel of switches. As she flicked on the lights, the store came to life. The shadows were gone, and the mannequins were just mannequins again.

Soon the store began to come to life in other ways. First the cleaning crew arrived. Then office workers trickled in. It seemed that every single person stopped to say good morning to Mama. Mama introduced every employee to Mia and Ricky by name. To each one she said proudly, "Look who accompanied me to work today!"

And every worker smiled back.

Mama showed Ricky and Mia the books she used to order merchandise for the store. They made a wish list of things they thought people their age would buy. While they worked, Mama's phone rang constantly. Some workers had called in sick. Mama looked at the schedule and helped find replacements. Other phone calls were questions, and Mama, the manager, always seemed to know the answers.

Just before it was time for Mama to open the store, Jeff, whose job was to supervise the stockroom, appeared in the office door. He was carrying a carton with a bit of grime on it. The carton was so big that only Jeff's head showed over the top. But the carton didn't cover the ear-to-ear grin on Jeff's face.

"They're here!" Jeff shouted, and Mama grinned back. "There are plenty more where these came from."

"What's in that box?" Mia and Ricky asked in chorus together.

In answer, Mama held up a funny looking little toy. It was a Teeny Tiny Tyke. Mia and Ricky recognized it right away even though they had never seen one up close. The toy was the latest fad that was sweeping the country. And these were the first Teeny Tiny Tykes in town.

"Thank goodness you two are here to help out," Jeff said to the twins. "It looks as if we're in for a really busy day!"

Mama made some quick decisions and sprang into action.

"Jeff, we'll need to set up displays right away. Put a few displays near each door, but spread the rest through the store so we don't have a mob scene. Set up tables beside the cash registers. I'll let security know we'll be busy today, and I'll have someone call in some extra salesclerks. Oh, and be sure we have plenty of change ready.

"Ricky and Mia, you're working for Jeff now. Ricky, help Jeff unpack the boxes and count the merchandise. Mia, you can set up the displays. Jeff will tell you where. Then you can both help Jeff keep the displays filled."

"But Mama," Mia asked, "what's all the excitement about? Nobody knows the Teeny Tiny Tykes are here. There was no ad in the paper. It won't be that busy."

Both Jeff and Mama turned to look at Mia. "Wait and see," they laughed.

Ricky and Mia did as they were told, but they really didn't see what all the fuss was about. Still, they worked quickly to show Mama and her co-workers that they had a good attitude.

Ricky opened boxes. Then he checked the packing slip and counted the pieces. Jeff began setting up tables. Beside each table, he stacked a few opened cartons. Mia took out Teeny Tiny Tykes, one at a time. Soon she finished arranging the first two displays. Not one customer had stopped by.

"Just as I predicted," Mia thought. "All this fuss was for nothing."

But as Mia began to work on the display by the mall door, something strange happened. A customer who was hurrying past stopped in her tracks. She gave a little scream and stared at the toys Mia was arranging.

"Peg! Dottie!" the woman called to some friends who were looking at a display in the mall window. "Look! They're here! The Teeny Tiny Tykes are here!"

All over the mall heads swiveled. People who had been walking by quietly moments before turned and flooded through the door. In just a few minutes, Mia was surrounded. Ricky, who was bringing out another box, got caught in the crowd too. Mia and Ricky upended the box and tossed the little toys onto the table in a heap. They turned to escape, but they were trapped! The noise was deafening.

"Ooh, aren't they cute!"

"I'll take them all."

"Do you have any more?"

Just at the right time, Mama appeared. She moved through the crowd, calming the customers and directing them to other displays throughout the store. Then she reached for Ricky and Mia and steered them to the edge of the mob.

As Mia and Ricky watched, Mama calmly cleared up the confusion. She reassured frantic customers that there were plenty of Teeny Tiny Tykes throughout the store and called over extra salesclerks to open all the nearby cash registers.

When she spotted a little girl crying at the edge of the mob, she led her to the table and helped her find just the right Teeny Tiny Tyke. Then she walked with the little girl to the cash register to make sure the clerk noticed her in the crowd of adults.

Mia saw a customer touch Mama's arm. The man looked cranky. "My grandmother just went into the hospital. She needs this warm robe right now. But there are so many people buying these dumb toys that I can't even get a salesclerk to notice me. And I'm in a hurry!"

Mia thought the customer's attitude was very rude, but Mama just smiled. She led the customer to an empty cash register, rang up the robe, and wrapped it in a pretty box. As the customer walked toward the door he was smiling.

"These little toys are kind of cute," the customer grinned.

Ricky and Mia had been standing off to the side watching Mama in action. Thanks to Mama, things were beginning to return to normal. The store was busy, but not frantic. Customers were smiling and chatting as they sorted through the toys. More customers were moving quickly through the checkout line. The clerks didn't look nervous any more. They smiled as Mama went to each one and quietly said, "Good job!"

Then Mama turned her attention to Ricky and Mia.

"I don't believe what I just saw," Ricky cried. "Those Teeny Tiny Tykes caused a reaction that spread like an infection."

"And you were like the doctor who cured it," Mia added.

"Just call me Dr. Mom," Mama joked. "But this day's not over yet. To keep things running smoothly, you two need to get back to work. Keep those Teeny Tiny Tykes coming!"

Mia and Ricky groaned, but they headed for the stockroom.

At five o'clock, Ricky and Mia collapsed on the chairs in Mama's office. They were tired and felt covered with grime from moving dusty boxes. They were proud too.

"Let's go home," they chimed.

But Mama still had a few more things to do. The night crew had just come on, and Mama wanted to make sure everything was in place. Ricky and Mia followed tiredly as Mama walked through the whole store, speaking to the employees and straightening displays.

As they neared the door, Mama said, "You two did a great job. Would you like some Teeny Tiny Tykes as a reward?"

"No, thanks!" Ricky and Mia groaned. They hurried outside. Mama just laughed.

After dinner, Mia and Ricky sat down at the kitchen table to work on their reports.

"I never realized how hard Mama works," Mia began.

"Or how important her job is," added Ricky.

Ricky opened his notebook to his report. This is what he wrote.

Mama is a manager at Block's Department Store. She works very hard and her job is important. She helps people in our town get the things they want and need. When there's a problem at the store, Mama finds a solution. Mama's positive attitude helps the whole store run smoothly. I'm glad I accompanied her to work. I certainly have a new respect for her work at the store. (I always knew she was a great Mom at home!)